NATIONAL GEOGRAPHIC KIDS

EVERYTHING
WEATHER

NATIONAL GEOGRAPHIC

EVERYTHING WEATHER

BY KATHY FURGANG

with National Geographic Explorer Tim Samaras

NATIONAL
GEOGRAPHIC

WASHINGTON, D.C.

CONTENTS

At the International Kite Festival, wind lifts this kite up into the sky above Durdham Downs, Bristol, England, in the United Kingdom.

5

INTRODUCTION

A CRASH OF THUNDER

JOLTS YOU FROM YOUR SLEEP! Lightning flashes. Rain pounds against the window. The wind howls. You pull the covers up to your chin and imagine what it's like to be outside. Lucky you! You're inside where it's warm and dry. As you begin to fall back to sleep, you wonder if you'll need an umbrella tomorrow. See? You're already a weather expert. You know that the weather can affect your life. Imagine if we thought mysterious forces controlled the weather. Like many ancient peoples, we would live in fear that the rain god would release deadly floods that could destroy our homes. Or the sun god wouldn't bring relief from winter's icy grip.

Today, we understand how weather works, but the forces that create it are still powerful and uncontrollable. We rely on the sun, rain, and wind to survive, but when weather turns bad, it can seriously mess up our lives. Tornadoes, hurricanes, monsoons, floods, and blizzards can not only wreck plans but also flatten houses and towns. Droughts, freezes, and hailstorms can destroy crops and property. Weather seriously affects your life and the world around you. So let's raise the temperature in here and learn EVERYTHING about weather!

EXPLORER'S CORNER

Hi! I'm Tim Samaras.

I guess you can say that I love wild weather. My specialty is chasing tornadoes and learning more about these beastly storms. I'm the guy running toward the tornado when everyone else is seeking cover. It can be a dangerous business, but I collect a lot of valuable information that helps us learn about tornadoes and how they form.

Candy-colored rainbows form during rain showers. The sunlight refracts, or changes direction, when it encounters the falling raindrops, creating gorgeous bands of color. You have a better chance of seeing a rainbow if you stand with the sun at your back.

WHAT'S THE WEATHER?

WEATHER... OR NOT?

EVERYBODY TALKS ABOUT IT,

BUT WHAT IS WEATHER? Weather is the condition of the air or atmosphere. Weather is constantly changing. Temperatures rise and fall. Air warms and cools. Wind can be fast or slow. Water in the air can take the form of fog, mist, rain, hail, snow, or sleet. All these things combined make up the weather. Weather can be crazy and unpredictable.

Run! Tornadoes can travel up to 70 miles per hour (113 kph). The average speed is 10 to 20 mph (16-32 kph). They don't travel very far on the ground. Few cover more than 6 miles (10 km).

Whoosh! The fastest wind on record **blew** 231 miles per hour (372 kph) on Mount Washington, New Hampshire, U.S.A., in 1934.

Zap! The Empire State Building in New York City **is struck by lightning** an average of **60 times a year.**

GIMME SHELTER

You're not the only one who needs shelter from a storm. Where do all the animals go when the weather turns bad? To hide from extreme temperatures, many animals dig a hole in the ground. The dirt cools their bodies in the summer and protects them from cold and ice in the winter. When hiding from rain, they're just like you. They never bring an umbrella, so they run for cover until the rain stops!

A mushroom makes a natural umbrella for this frog.

WHAT ISN'T WEATHER?

IT ISN'T SEASONAL CHANGE.

Hot summers and cold winters are related to weather, but seasonal changes happen because of climate. Weather is the minute-to-minute changes in the atmosphere. Climate is how the atmosphere changes over a long period of time, such as during one yearly cycle. Many scientists believe that the Earth's climate is changing due to human activities, such as pollution. They argue that climate change is one of the most serious problems facing humans today.

IT ISN'T CHANGES IN EARTH'S CRUST.

Earthquakes and volcanoes are not part of the weather. These events create landforms and shift Earth's plates. They don't cause weather either. Weather happens in the air, not on or under the ground or ocean.

WEATHER ALERT   A RAINDROP TYPICALLY FALLS AT A SPEED OF 17 MILES PER HOUR (27 KPH).

HERE COMES THE SUN

THE SUN IS EARTH'S FIVE-BILLION-YEAR-OLD FRIEND.

HOW HOT IS IT? Really hot! The sun has a core of gases that reaches a temperature of 27 million degrees Fahrenheit (or 15 million degrees Celsius). Here on Earth, we are 93 million miles (150 million km) away from the sun, but that's still close enough to feel the burn. The sun provides most of the heat and light for the planet, but it is not the only factor in the weather.

All those millions of miles from the sun, our planet spins on an axis. The rotation causes moving air to change direction. Add more movement to air that is rising, falling, and changing temperatures, and you end up with a wild weather ride.

When it comes to causing weather, the sun, land, and air are partners. The sun heats large patches of land, which warm the air above them. The wind then moves the warm air around, sometimes bumping cooler patches out of the way. The air's constant shifting, rising, falling, heating, and cooling make the weather very unpredictable.

SUNSCREEN, ANYONE?

Sunlight is natural, so how can it be bad for you? The sun batters us daily with its rays. Ultraviolet, or UV, rays can cause a painful sunburn and other serious problems. Luckily, you can fight UV rays with sunscreen. The letters *SPF* on the bottle stand for Sun Protection Factor. SPF 30 blocks out 96.7 percent of UV rays. Slather it on to stay safe.

EXOSPHERE
372 miles (600 km) and beyond
The exosphere extends out into outer space. Satellites orbit in the lower exosphere.

LIFE UNDER PRESSURE

Feel that? Here on Earth, the air presses against us with a force of about 15 pounds per square inch (or 1,013.25 x 10 dynes per sq km). You can't really feel atmospheric pressure, but it does play a role in weather prediction.

Weather takes place in the region of the atmosphere closest to Earth's surface, called the troposphere. That is where the air pressure is highest.

We can predict weather changes by measuring air pressure with a tool called a barometer. When air pressure rises, fair weather is on its way. When air pressure falls, rainy or stormy weather might follow.

THERMOSPHERE
53-372 miles high (85-600 km) Space shuttles orbit here. The southern and northern lights occur here.

MESOSPHERE
31-53 miles high (50-85 km) Meteors burn up here.

STRATOSPHERE
9-31 miles high (15-50 km) Airplanes and weather balloons fly here.

TROPOSPHERE
0-9 miles high (0-15 km) Most weather happens here.

WEATHER ALERT
ESCAPED GASES FROM THE SUN TRAVEL AT A MILLION MILES PER HOUR (1,609,000 KPH).

SEND IN THE CLOUDS

HOW MUCH DOES A CLOUD WEIGH?

A light, fluffy, cumulus cloud typically weighs about 216,000 pounds (97,975 kg). That's about the weight of 18 elephants. A rain-soaked cumulonimbus cloud typically weighs 105.8 million pounds (48,000,000 kg), or about 9,000 elephants.

CLOUDS CAN BE NAUGHTY OR NICE.

WILL THEY SIGNAL A SUNNY DAY OR WILL THEY RAIN ON your parade? If you want a clue about the weather, look up at the clouds. They'll tell a lot about the condition of the air and what weather might be on the way. Clouds are made of both air and water. On fair days, warm air currents rise up and push against the water in clouds, keeping it from falling. But as the raindrops in a cloud get bigger, it's time to set them free. The bigger raindrops become too heavy for the air currents to hold up, and they fall to the ground.

NAUGHTY
Stratus clouds

NICE
Cumulus clouds

WEATHER ALERT   FOG IS ACTUALLY A STRATUS CLOUD THAT FORMS NEAR THE GROUND.

CIRRUS

These wispy tufts of clouds are thin and hang high up in the atmosphere where the air is extremely cold. Cirrus clouds are made of tiny ice crystals.

I CAN BE NAUGHTY OR NICE! A storm is on its way (boo!), or a storm is nearly over (hooray!).

CUMULONIMBUS

These are the monster clouds. Rising air currents force fluffy cumulus clouds to swell and shoot upward, as much as 70,000 feet (21,000 m). When these clouds bump against the top of the troposphere, or the tropopause, they flatten out on top like tabletops.

I'M NAUGHTY! Run for cover! I might rain or hail on you.

CIRROSTRATUS

CIRROCUMULUS

ALTOSTRATUS

ALTOCUMULUS

STRATOCUMULUS

CUMULUS

These white, fluffy clouds make people sing, "Oh, what a beautiful morning!" They form low in the atmosphere and look like marshmallows. They often mix with large patches of blue sky. Formed when hot air rises, cumulus clouds usually disappear when the air cools at night.

I'M NICE! Good weather is coming, but watch out if I change my shape!

STRATUS

These clouds make the sky look like a bowl of thick gray porridge. They hang low in the sky, blanketing the day in dreary darkness. Stratus clouds form when cold, moist air close to the ground moves over a region.

I'M NAUGHTY! Grab your umbrella because it's going to rain.

NIMBOSTRATUS

EXPLORER'S CORNER

I'm always on the lookout for some good cumulonimbus clouds. They're the clouds that produce tornadoes, which are the heart of my research. I check my radar for some rotating clouds that could produce a funnel cloud that reaches the ground. A funnel cloud is made up of dust, water droplets, and any debris it picks up as it rotates near the ground.

THE SKY IS FALLING

THE SKY CAN'T **ACTUALLY FALL, BUT MOISTURE** IN THE AIR **CAN AND DOES.**

PRECIPITATION IS A FANCY WORD
FOR THE WET STUFF THAT FALLS FROM THE SKY.

Precipitation is rain, freezing rain, sleet, snow, or hail. It forms when water vapor in the air condenses into clouds, gets heavier, and drops to the ground. Precipitation can ruin a picnic, but life on Earth couldn't exist without it.

SLEET
Develops when ice crystals fall toward the ground, partly melt, and then refreeze. This happens mainly in winter when air near the ground is below freezing temperatures.

RAIN
Formed when ice crystals in high, cold clouds get heavy and fall. Even in summer, falling ice crystals could remain frozen, but warm air near the ground melts them into raindrops.

FREEZING RAIN
Falls during the winter when rain freezes immediately as it hits a surface. Freezing rain creates layers of ice on the roads and causes dangerous driving conditions.

WEATHER ALERT   THE AVERAGE HAILSTONE IS THE SIZE OF A FOUR-YEAR-OLD'S FINGERNAIL.

HAIL

Formed inside thunderstorms when ice crystals covered in water pass through patches of freezing air in the tops of cumulonimbus clouds. The water on the ice crystals freezes. The crystals become heavy and fall to the ground.

TAKING EARTH'S TEMPERATURE

The United States uses the English system, or Fahrenheit measurement, to describe temperature. Much of the rest of the world uses the metric system, or Celsius measurement. The temperature is the same, but it's just expressed differently. For example, 75°F in Seattle, Washington, U.S.A., is 23°C in Vancouver, British Columbia, Canada. How do you know? Just do the math.

Here's how to convert Fahrenheit to Celsius:
- Subtract 32, multiply by 5, and then divide by 9.
  Example: 55°F equals how many degrees Celsius?
  $(55-32) \times 5 \div 9 = 13°C$

Now let's go the other way—from Celsius to Fahrenheit:
- Multiply by 9, divide by 5, and then add 32.

SNOW

Produced when ice crystals in clouds get heavy enough to fall. The air has to be cold enough all the way down for the crystals to stay frozen.

PRECIPITATION NUMBERS

0 inches is the amount of rain on record in the Antofagasta Region of the Atacama Desert in Chile. It never rains there.

8 inches (20 cm) is the diameter of the world's largest known hailstone. (July 2010, South Dakota)

12 inches (30.5 cm) is the most rainfall recorded in one hour in the U.S. (June 22, 1947, Holt, Missouri)

72 inches (183 cm) of rainfall is the most ever recorded during a 24-hour period. (January 8, 1966, the French island Reunion, during Tropical Cyclone Denise)

118 days is the longest recorded amount of time without rain in the United States. (Ending June 1, 2011, El Paso, Texas)

1,042 inches (27 m) is the most rainfall recorded in one year. (1860–1861, Cherrapunji, India)

A PHOTOGRAPHIC DIAGRAM

THE WATER CYCLE

SCIENTISTS THINK THAT

THE WATER WE DRINK, BATHE IN, AND USE TO GROW CROPS today has been here on Earth since long before the time of the dinosaurs. It has just been moving around and around in the atmosphere in a nearly endless cycle. Earth has a limited supply of water. It's a good thing, then, that Mother Nature created the water cycle—Earth's original recycling project. Here's how it works:

RISING UP

Some of the water and spray from this moving waterfall will **evaporate** into the air. In other bodies of water, heat from the sun causes some water to evaporate, or turn into water vapor, or gas. This water vapor rises from the stream, river, or lake and goes into the air.

HANGING OUT

Water covers over 70 percent of Earth's surface in the form of oceans, lakes, and rivers. When water ends up on land from rain, snow, or hail, it will either soak up into the earth and become part of the groundwater that animals and plants drink, or it will collect in bodies of water.

CHILLING OUT

As water vapor cools in the air, it **condenses.** This means that it changes back into liquid form. You will notice the same kind of thing happening if you pour a cold glass of water on a hot day. Water forms on the outside of the glass. The water vapor in the warm air touches the cold glass and turns to liquid.

FALLING DOWN

After so much water has condensed that the air can't hold it anymore, it falls as **precipitation**—rain, hail, sleet, or snow—into Earth's oceans, lakes, and rivers.

RUNNING OFF

Some precipitation leaves the cycle briefly. Melted snow and rain that run downhill eventually end up in large bodies of water. The transfer of land water to the ocean is called **runoff.**

Located at the border of China and Vietnam, the Detian Waterfall is one of the largest waterfalls in Asia. Its name means "virtuous heaven."

Hurricanes often bring storm surges, or rises in sea level of up to 20 feet (6 m). Storm surges are huge walls of water that charge toward coastal land, with the power to destroy everything in their path.

2
WEATHER EXTREMES

DANGEROUS WEATHER

POWERFUL FORCES
OF NATURE CAN LEAD TO
severe weather—dangerous acts of nature that put people, animals, and buildings at risk. Let's take a bird's eye view of some of the world's most serious weather events.

HURRICANES

Hurricanes are storms with high winds and heavy rain. They start as tropical storms that form over warm ocean waters. Once a tropical storm reaches 74 miles per hour (119 kph), it becomes a hurricane—a circular storm with a distinct spiral shape and a clearly defined eye at its center. Not all hurricanes reach landfall. Many stay out at sea where they cause little damage. Hurricanes in the Northern Hemisphere turn in a counterclockwise direction; those in the Southern Hemisphere turn clockwise.

WEATHER ALERT   HURRICANES, TYPHOONS, AND CYCLONES ARE ALL TROPICAL STORMS.

FLOODS

Floods occur when too much rain forces streams, rivers, and lakes to overflow. After excessive rain or snowmelt, rivers and streams steadily rise along their banks until the water finds a weak spot and breaks through.

A flash flood, however, can happen in a matter of minutes. Flash floods occur when heavy rains fall on areas of hard, dry ground. Streams, rivers, and creeks fill up fast until the water bursts from the beds.

THUNDER AND LIGHTNING STORMS

Thunder and lightning storms are the most common form of extreme weather. Thunderstorm clouds produce strong, sudden movements of air, which cause water drops and pieces of ice in the storm to collide, break apart, and form positive and negative charges. The difference in charge causes electrical energy to build up. It is discharged in the form of lightning.

BLIZZARDS

Blizzards are storms with blowing or falling snow, high winds, and very cold temperatures. Blizzard conditions occur when high winds of 35 miles per hour (56 kph) or higher push the snow around for more than three hours.

DROUGHTS

Droughts are serious weather events. Droughts occur when an area does not get enough seasonal rainfall or snowmelt. As a result, the area's water supplies shrink. Droughts can affect large geographic areas and have serious long-term effects on the land. Droughts can dry up creeks, rivers, and lakes; kill trees; and ruin crops, gardens, and lawns. Drought conditions also make wildfires more likely when lightning strikes the dry ground.

WIND SCALE

This scale, which was developed by wind engineer Herb Saffir and meteorologist Bob Simpson, helps weather-watchers understand the severity of a coming hurricane.

Saffir-Simpson Hurricane Scale

Category	Wind Speed
1	**74-95 mph** (119-152 kph) **Dangerous winds, some damage**
2	**96-110 mph** (154-177 kph) **Extremely dangerous winds, extensive damage**
3	**111-130 mph** (178-209 kph) **Devastating damage**
4	**131-155 mph** (210-249 kph) **Catastrophic damage**
5	**More than 155 mph** (249 kph) **Catastrophic damage**

WHAT IS A TORNADO?

TORNADOES, ALSO KNOWN
AS TWISTERS, ARE FUNNELS OF RAPIDLY ROTATING AIR
that are created during a thunderstorm. With wind speeds of up to 200 mph (482 kph), tornadoes have the power to pick up and destroy everything in their path.

SUPERCELL

A massive rotating thunderstorm that generates the most destructive of all tornadoes. A series of supercells in the southern United States caused an outbreak of 92 tornadoes in ten states over a 15-hour period in 2008.

WEATHER ALERT TORNADOES HAVE OCCURRED IN ALL 50 U.S. STATES AND ON EVERY CONTINENT EXCEPT ANTARCTICA.

FIRE WHIRLS

Tornadoes made of wind and fire that occur during a wildfire. These flaming towers can be five to ten stories tall and can last for more than an hour. They are also called fire whirls or fire devils.

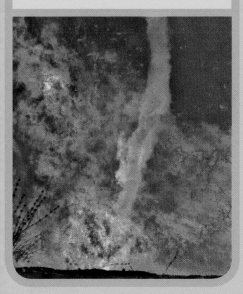

TORNADO FAMILY

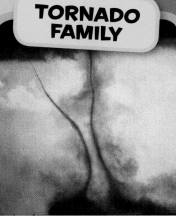

Two to three tornadoes, which can run linear, parallel, or even intersecting paths at the same time. They are usually spawned by a supercell thunderstorm.

FUNNEL CLOUD

A rotating funnel of air formed in a cumulus or cumulonimbus cloud that becomes a tornado if it touches the ground

WATERSPOUT

A waterspout is a funnel-shaped column that forms over water and is usually weaker than a land tornado.

THE FUJITA SCALE

The Enhanced Fujita (EF) Scale, named after tornado expert Tetsuya Fujita, classifies tornadoes based on wind speed and the intensity of damage that they cause.

EF0
65-85 mph winds
(105-137 kph)
Slight damage

EF1
86-110 mph winds
(138-177 kph)
Moderate damage

EF2
111-135 mph winds
(179-217 kph)
Substantial damage

EF3
136-165 mph winds
(219-266 kph)
Severe damage

EF4
166-200 mph winds
(267-322 kph)
Massive damage

EF5
More than 200 mph winds
(322 kph)
Catastrophic damage

FREAKY
WEATHER

THERE'S BAD WEATHER,
AND THEN THERE'S FREAKY WEATHER—
weather events so bizarre, unexpected, and rare that people are always amazed to see them. Here are some of Mother Nature's odd weather events and some possible explanations.

RAINING FROGS AND FISH

What are people to think when the sky turns dark but instead of raindrops, frogs and fish fall from the sky? One possible explanation is a waterspout. When a waterspout forms over a body of water, the force of the whirling funnel cloud sucks up small creatures, such as fish and frogs. When the cloud moves over land, it then loses energy, and the critters come tumbling down.

NORTHERN LIGHTS

In places at high latitudes, such as Norway and Australia, you can sometimes see curtains of colored light in the sky. The northern lights and southern lights are caused when energized particles leave the sun and collide miles above Earth, giving off bursts of colored light.

WEATHER ALERT   A LIGHTNING BOLT CAN REACH TEMPERATURES OF UP TO 50,000°F (28,000°C).

SNOW ROLLERS

Snow rollers form when sticky, loose snow lies on the ground at just below freezing. Add a steady breeze, and you might end up with a snow roller. Most are about 12 inches (30 cm) in diameter.

EXPLORER'S CORNER

What makes weather freaky? It's unpredictable and unexpected. Nature always seems to be doing something that surprises and even scares us. My passion for storms has always been driven by the beautiful and powerful storms that occur in the midwestern U.S. each spring. For other people, it's the storm surges that develop near land before a hurricane hits. Everyone has a different experience with the weather. For me, my interest started when I was about six years old and saw that fantastic tornado in *The Wizard of Oz*. Now *that's* some freaky weather. Weather is an inspiration for many people. When we experience amazing weather firsthand, we never forget it.

FIRE RAINBOW

When sunlight bends through ice crystals in high cirrus clouds, a fire rainbow might appear. Fire rainbows don't form in a regular shape like other rainbows. Instead, they look like candy-colored flames flickering up in the clouds. The conditions needed to form a fire rainbow are so exact that witnesses consider themselves lucky to see one.

BALL LIGHTNING

A mysterious weather event, ball lightning takes the form of a small glowing globe. Unlike a white lightning bolt, ball lightning may be red, orange, blue, or yellow. Witnesses say that ball lightning makes a hissing sound and leaves behind an odd smell. Ball lightning travels fast—a quick flash that is often, but not always, followed by an explosion. Because ball lightning happens so unexpectedly and so quickly, it has not been well documented or studied.

WILD WEATHER ZONES

EXTREME WEATHER

TAKES PLACE ALL OVER THE WORLD, BUT SOME TYPES OF POWERFUL STORMS TEND to occur in the same places over and over again. Seasonal wind currents and air and water temperatures near these zones shape the storms. Take a look at the world map below to see where wild weather likes to go.

NORTH AMERICA

Caribbean Sea

SOUTH AMERICA

TORNADOES

Tornadoes are most common in the United States. The flatland from the Great Plains to Texas provides the perfect landing strip for twisters. This stretch is known as Tornado Alley. Still, many destructive tornadoes have occurred in areas outside the Alley.

TROPICAL STORMS

Hurricanes form over warm tropical waters. As a result, they are most likely to strike coastal areas. The Eastern Pacific hurricane season runs from May 15 to November 30. The Atlantic hurricane season lasts from June 1 to November 30. Hurricanes are called cyclones in the South Pacific and Indian Ocean, and typhoons in Japan, China, and the Philippines.

LONGES
DROUG
Atacama D
Chile, 400

WEATHER ALERT   U.S. WEATHER FORECASTS ARE ACCURATE ABOUT 85 PERCENT OF THE TIME.

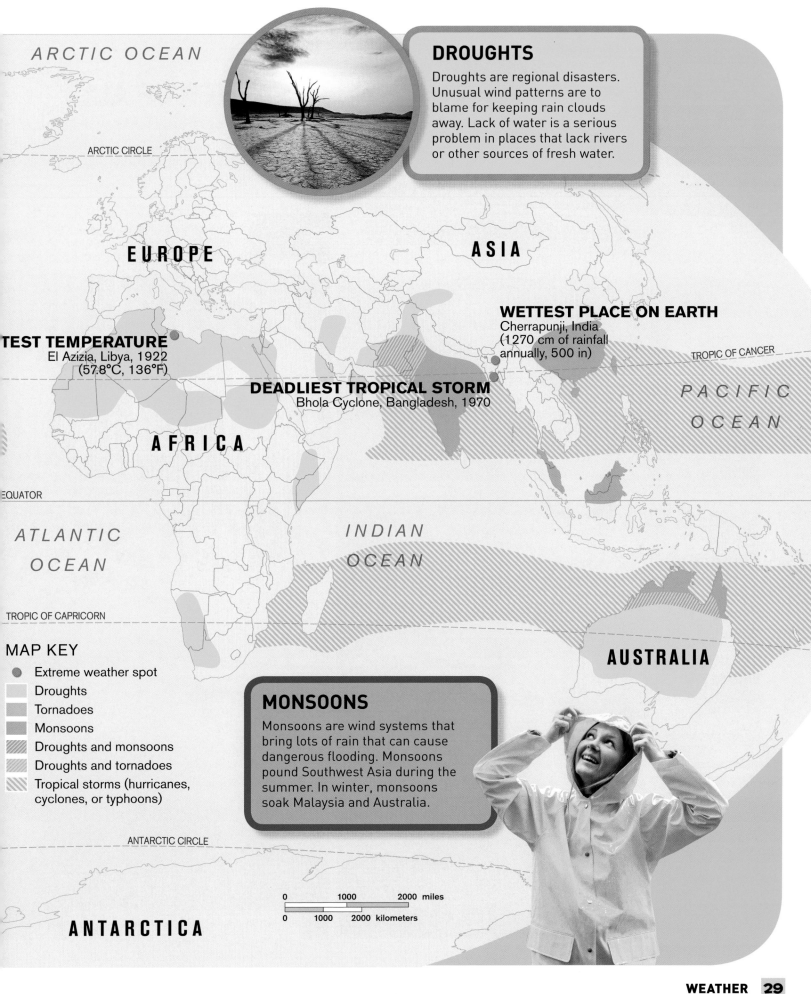

DROUGHTS

Droughts are regional disasters. Unusual wind patterns are to blame for keeping rain clouds away. Lack of water is a serious problem in places that lack rivers or other sources of fresh water.

ARCTIC OCEAN

ARCTIC CIRCLE

EUROPE

ASIA

WETTEST PLACE ON EARTH
Cherrapunji, India
(1270 cm of rainfall annually, 500 in)

TROPIC OF CANCER

TEST TEMPERATURE
El Azizia, Libya, 1922
(57.8°C, 136°F)

DEADLIEST TROPICAL STORM
Bhola Cyclone, Bangladesh, 1970

PACIFIC
OCEAN

AFRICA

EQUATOR

ATLANTIC
OCEAN

INDIAN
OCEAN

TROPIC OF CAPRICORN

AUSTRALIA

MAP KEY
● Extreme weather spot
  Droughts
  Tornadoes
  Monsoons
  Droughts and monsoons
  Droughts and tornadoes
  Tropical storms (hurricanes, cyclones, or typhoons)

MONSOONS

Monsoons are wind systems that bring lots of rain that can cause dangerous flooding. Monsoons pound Southwest Asia during the summer. In winter, monsoons soak Malaysia and Australia.

ANTARCTIC CIRCLE

| 0 | 1000 | 2000 miles |
| 0 | 1000 | 2000 kilometers |

ANTARCTICA

A PHOTO GALLERY

WEATHER OF ALL

TYPES CAN BE BEAUTIFUL. Weather events are just one more opportunity for Mother Nature to show off her talents. Take a look for yourself!

At Hurricane Ridge in Washington State's Olympic National Park, in the U.S., icicles form when snow begins to melt and then temperatures fall again.

Madagascar is an island off the coast of Africa. During a drought, a dust storm swept in, forcing people and livestock away from the area.

The pebbled beaches of Hampshire, England, in the United Kingdom, are the site of some amazing sunsets.

A thick fog sets in over the Restigouche River in Quebec, Canada. Fog like this is most common early in the morning, before the sun is high in the sky.

Lightning strikes over the ocean are rare. The lightning fans out because the water acts as a conductor.

This lion has little protection from sandstorms in South Africa's Kalahari Gemsbok National Park.

These rock formations in the Wadi Rayan, southwest of Cairo, Egypt, were shaped by the forces of wind and rain. During the rainy season, this area fills with water.

When the light and the clouds are just right, you can sometimes see bands of rain falling, as here in Chihuahua, Mexico.

Modern weather forecasters use computers to predict the weather, but they still rely on weather balloons to collect raw data. The balloons were first invented in 1896. Now about 900 weather balloons get released around the world every day. They travel 20 miles (32 km) into the air to get the information weather predictors need.

3
WEATHER PREDICTIONS

WEATHER-WATCHING PAST AND PRESENT

FOR CENTURIES, PEOPLE DIDN'T
UNDERSTAND HOW WEATHER WORKED. THEY THOUGHT

powerful forces were in control, so people made offerings to gods in hopes that the gods would grant good weather. Over time, they used their observations of the sky and clouds to predict the weather—"Clear moon, frost soon"—but they weren't very accurate. In the mid-1600s, scientists finally developed the basic tools of modern weather prediction, the thermometer and the barometer. From then on, weather-watchers kept records and noticed trends using these instruments. Weather prediction became more reliable, but nature still had the advantage.

It wasn't until well into the 20th century that scientists had the data and technology to predict the weather with much accuracy. Plus, engineering techniques are improving constantly. We can't control the weather, but we can make more accurate predictions and take steps that save more lives.

In the first half of the 20th century, for example, storms sometimes made the Thames River overflow into London, England, in the United Kingdom. In 1982, engineers completed the Thames Barrier. One of the largest moveable flood barriers in the world, it is considered an engineering marvel! Even today, ever-changing weather keeps challenging meteorologists and engineers to come up with the next big idea.

The Thames Barrier

BY THE NUMBERS

4 is the most Category 5 hurricanes on record in one Atlantic hurricane season. (2005)

6 is the number of months in the Atlantic hurricane season.

136 degrees Fahrenheit (58°C) is the highest temperature recorded. (Libya, 1922)

226 is the greatest number of tornadoes in a 24-hour period. (United States, April 27-28, 2011)

WEATHER ALERT
COUNT THE CHIRPS A CRICKET MAKES IN 15 SECONDS. ADD 37 TO FIND THE TEMPERATURE IN FAHRENHEIT.

A SHOCKING DISCOVERY

Ben Franklin, an early American statesman and inventor, used a kite to determine that lightning was a form of electricity. In June 1752, he built a kite from wooden sticks, a silk handkerchief, and some twine. He attached a wire antenna to the kite and a metal key to the string, and released the contraption into storm clouds above a field. Lightning struck the wire and traveled through the kite and string to the key. When Franklin touched the key with his hand, he received a jolt. (Don't try this yourself!) Afterward, Franklin placed a lightning rod on his roof and attached it by wires to a bell. When lightning struck, the bell would ring.

WEATHER THAT MADE HISTORY

Bad weather can mess up a picnic, but can it ruin a battle or a shuttle launch? As you know, not even generals and scientists can control the weather. Read about three important historical events that were affected by the weather.

***ATLANTIS* SPACE LAUNCH** The atmospheric conditions for NASA's space shuttle launches in Florida had to be just right—clear and cloudless. Delays due to cloudy or stormy weather were common. Just two days before the final launch of the U.S. space shuttle *Atlantis,* weather forecasters predicted a 70 percent chance of cancellation due to a stormy weather system. But weather, as you know, can change quickly, and it did that day. The final launch took place on July 8, 2011, right on schedule.

THE BATTLE OF NORMANDY The "D-Day" invasion of Normandy, France, helped turn the tide during World War II, but it almost didn't happen because of the weather. For weeks before the battle, the weather was so horrendous that the invasion had to be delayed from late May until early June. Despite continuing rain, the momentous battle took place on June 6, 1944.

VALLEY FORGE The winter of 1777 was the lowest point of the American Revolution, and the weather did not help. George Washington's troops suffered terribly from freezing temperatures at Valley Forge, Pennsylvania. Many died or threatened to quit the army.

WEATHER SAYINGS

These observations got handed down as memorable sayings that you might still hear today. They aren't reliable. Check the weather report instead.
- Red sky in the morning, sailors take warning. Red sky at night, sailors' delight.
- Clear nights mean cold days.
- If a circle forms 'round the moon, then it will rain very soon.
- Rain before seven stops by eleven.
- In a green sky, the cows will fly.

TOOLS OF THE TRADE

NATIONAL WEATHER SERVICES AROUND THE WORLD HAVE BEEN KEEPING RECORDS SINCE THE LATE 1800s.

MODERN WEATHER FORECASTS

AREN'T PERFECT, BUT THEY HAVE PLENTY OF RELIABLE SCIENTIFIC information and technology to back them up. Check out the technology that meteorologists use to figure out if you need to bring your umbrella or smooth on the sunscreen.

WARM FRONTS show where the leading edge of a moving mass of warm air is.

COLD FRONTS show where the leading edge of a moving mass of cold air is.

ATMOSPHERIC PRESSURE Local areas of low pressure are indicated by the capital letter L.

OCCLUDED FRONTS show where two air masses come together, and one takes over the other. The occluded front shows where weather will change.

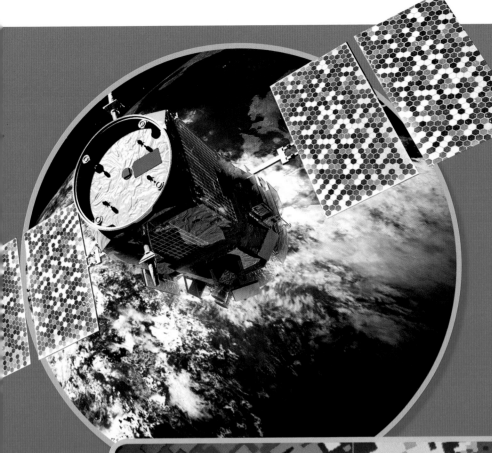

EYES IN THE SKIES

Weather satellites orbit the Earth and monitor weather events around the globe. They use thermal sensors to measure ocean water temperatures and track where weather events might be headed. They also see the tops of clouds and determine their type, height, and temperature. Satellites capture images of hurricanes that show the location of the eyes and observe their movements. The images are displayed on maps, with colors representing different temperature and moisture levels. Meteorologists read and interpret these images before issuing advisories, watches, or warnings when severe storms develop.

ON YOUR RADAR

Radar is an important weather prediction tool. Special dish-shaped antennas, located high up on towers all around the world, send out radio waves that bounce off moving objects in their path, such as wind or rain. When the waves encounter raindrops or winds, changes in their patterns tell meteorologists where the weather event is likely to go. These changes show up as different colors, as on this radar map. Objects moving toward an antenna have a higher wave frequency. Objects moving away from an antenna have a lower wave frequency.

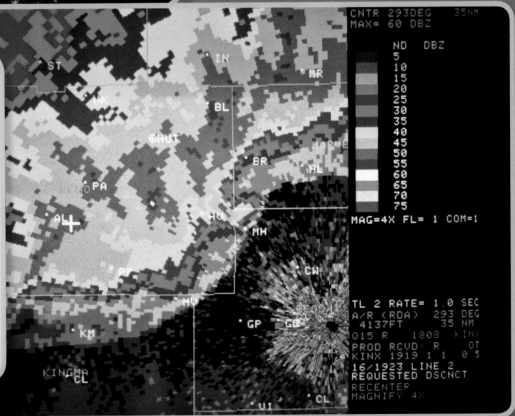

WEATHER ALERT DOPPLER RADAR IS SO SENSITIVE THAT IT CAN DETECT MOVEMENTS OF INSECTS OR DUST IN THE AIR.

DODGING DISASTERS

METEOROLOGISTS ISSUE DIFFERENT

FORECASTS WHEN A SERIOUS STORM APPROACHES. THE PURPOSE of the forecasts is to tell people how severe the weather may become. The U.S. National Weather Service (NWS) and the international World Weather Information Service (WWIS) both have three levels of warnings. Different words describe the levels, but both weather services use yellow, orange, and red to indicate increasing danger.

NWS	WWIS	
ADVISORY	BE AWARE	An advisory means that hazardous weather is occurring or likely to occur. People should be careful.
WATCH	BE PREPARED	A watch means "look out" because the risks of hazardous weather have greatly increased. People should have a plan for getting out of harm's way.
WARNING	TAKE ACTION	A warning means there is a significant threat to life and property. Be prepared and stay safe.

BE PREPARED!

Thanks to modern technology, we usually get a warning that severe weather is coming. People who live near the coast can protect their homes from dangerous hurricanes. Boarding up windows and sandbagging doors is one way to prepare. People who live in areas hit by tornadoes don't have much prep time. They must find a safe hiding place in their houses. The best choice is a small, windowless room on the lowest level of the house—the cellar, a bathroom, or a closet. If there's time, drag in a mattress and climb under it. Then hold on!

HIT THE ROAD

If storm warnings tell you to evacuate an area before a storm, then get out of town! You don't want to be stuck on your own during hazardous weather. You may think you can ride out a storm, but if you get into trouble, you will put your own life as well as the lives of rescue crews at risk. Don't do it!

HABOOB ON THE LOOSE

Haboobs are impressive dust storms that occur in desert regions of the world, including the Middle East, Australia, and the American Southwest. Meteorologists describe haboobs as "walls of dust" that form when a blast of cold air shoots out from the bottom of a thunderstorm cloud. The air hits the ground with an explosive punch, kicking up massive clouds of dirt and dust. These clouds get pushed along the ground at incredible speeds, up to 50 miles per hour (80 kph). A haboob is not a deadly storm, but you don't want to get caught up in one. The dust will make you cough and your eyes sting. Stay inside until it passes. Still, people caught in a haboob will need a bath, not a trip to the doctor.

WEATHER ALERT THE WORD "HABOOB" COMES FROM ARABIC, AND IT MEANS "BLOWING VIOLENTLY."

STORM CHASERS

STORM CHASERS RISK LIFE AND LIMB

TO GET DATA THAT HELP US LEARN ABOUT STORMS. Storm chasing is definitely not for wimps. It can be a complicated business, as dozens of people work together to find, chase, and document severe storms. Storm chasers take great risks to get information and snap dramatic photos and video of hurricanes, lightning, tornadoes, or hail storms that you may see on TV or in books like this one.

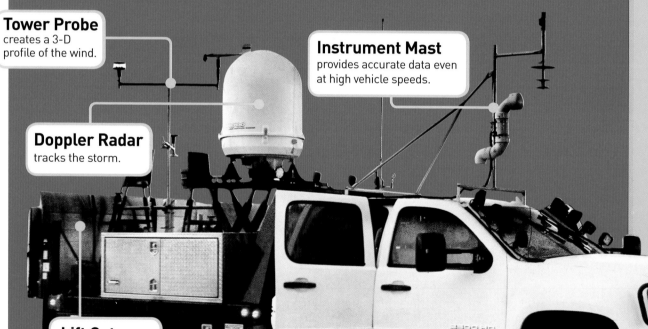

Tower Probe
creates a 3-D profile of the wind.

Instrument Mast
provides accurate data even at high vehicle speeds.

Doppler Radar
tracks the storm.

Lift Gate
lifts and places the 400-pound (181 kg) Tower Probe.

Front End includes an air compressor and an 8,000 pound (3,629 kg) capacity winch.

The Probe vehicle of Team Twistex

READY TO ROLL

A storm chaser's vehicle ha two important jobs—to carr tons of equipment and to keep the storm chasers saf As you can see, Tim Samar truck does both. It is loaded with equipment inside and out. On top are instruments for measuring and tracking the storm. Inside are compu ers, radios, scanners, and global positioning equipme The truck's body has been reinforced so that it can wit stand 200 mile-per-hour (32 kph) winds and 5-inch (12.7 cm) pieces of hail. The windows are made of bulletpro material that is transparent enough to allow storm chas to see and photograph the tornadoes.

WEATHER ALERT STORM CHASERS HUNT HUNDREDS OF TORNADOES IN TORNADO ALLEY, IN THE U.S., EACH YEAR.

Hurricane hunters such as Bill Olney got a real workout during Hurricane Irene, which caused billions of dollars in damage to the United States in August 2011.

DON'T TRY THIS AT HOME

Storm chasing is dangerous for everyone, including experts with years of experience, such as the one shown here. So DON'T try it on your own. If you are interested in learning about storm chasing as a career, contact your local National Weather Service bureau to find out about training courses in spotting storms and tracking severe weather. You can learn the safe way to watch a storm.

EXPLORER'S CORNER

When I chase a tornado, my goal is to place an electronic data-recording device called a probe in the path of the tornado. I designed the turtle probe to measure pressure inside tornadoes. In this 2003 photo, I was placing probes in the direct line of an EF4 tornado in Manchester, South Dakota. I was 100 yards (91 m) ahead of the approaching tornado. That's the closest I've been to a violent tornado! Debris was flying overhead, telephone poles were snapped and flung through the air, and roads got ripped from the ground. The tornado's path carved perfectly through a cornfield, where it mowed stalks down to the ground.

Video Probe records the storm with different camera angles.

WEATHER EVENTS
CAN BE SO BIG AND WIDESPREAD

that it's sometimes hard to comprehend them. For example, a single hurricane can cover hundreds of miles; its eye alone can be up to 200 miles wide (320 km). That's about as far as Paris, France, is from London, England, U.K. But weather is also a part of daily life. Let's think about weather in terms of some everyday objects and events.

WEATHER COMPARISONS

HOW MUCH? HOW MANY?

TORNADO SPEED
On the ground, a tornado can move between 10 and 20 miles per hour (16-32 kph). That's about as fast as the world's fastest marathon runner.

The average lightning bolt produces about 250 kilowatt-hours of electricity. That's enough to power a single household for two weeks.

IS IT HOT ENOUGH TO FRY AN EGG?

Sidewalks can get hot enough (158°F/70°C), but once an egg hits the surface, the sidewalk cools. The sun alone can't cook the egg thoroughly.

HOW FAST IS A HURRICANE?

According to the Saffir-Simpson scale, a Category 5 hurricane can reach winds of over 155 miles per hour (249 kph). That's about as fast as some race cars speed around the track.

HOW MUCH RAIN IN A SNOWFALL?

Snowflakes come in many different shapes and sizes so each snowfall contains a different amount of moisture. Rule of thumb: 10 inches (25 cm) of snow are equal to an inch (2.5 cm) of rain.

4

FUN
WITH
WEATHER

Sledding, skating, building snow sculptures, and catching snowflakes on your tongue are tons of fun in the frosty weather.

WEATHER DETECTIVE

USE WHAT **YOU'VE LEARNED** ABOUT WEATHER TO READ THE SKY AND MAKE PREDICTIONS.

HURRICANE NAME GAME

Meteorologists give hurricanes names so that the storms can be tracked more easily. During hurricane season, storms are named alphabetically and alternate between boys' and girls' names. The letters *Q, U, X, Y,* and *Z* are not used. Each year's list of names is drawn up long before the storms even form. What names would you give to hurricanes for the next season?

CLOUD JUMBLE

LET'S SEE HOW MUCH YOU'VE LEARNED about clouds. Look at each picture of a cloud. Match each cloud to its name. Here's the tricky part—the letters in the names are jumbled. Can you figure out the answers?

a. monilubsumcu

b. tarusts

c. muuslcu

d. ruiscr

1
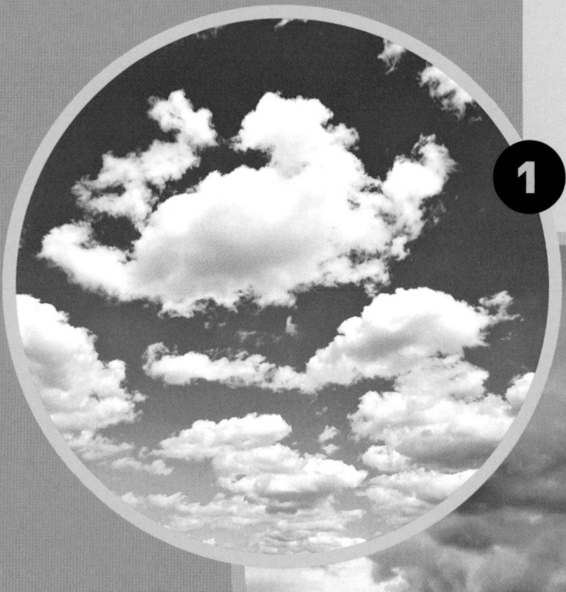

2
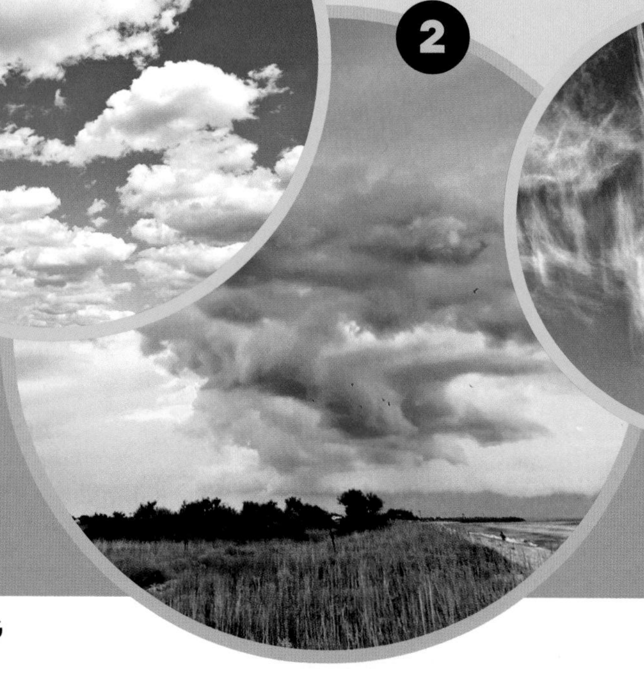

3
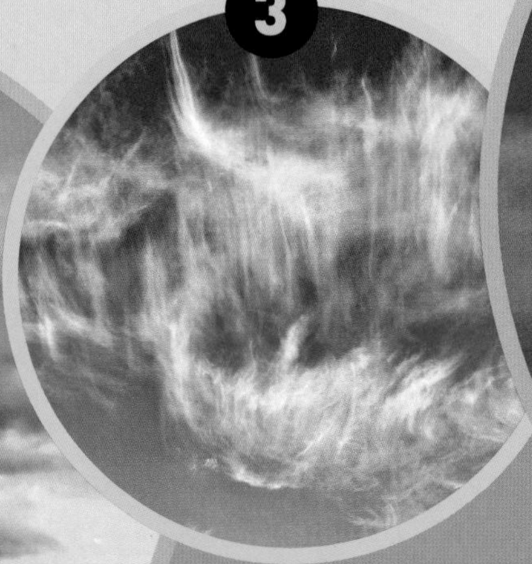

4
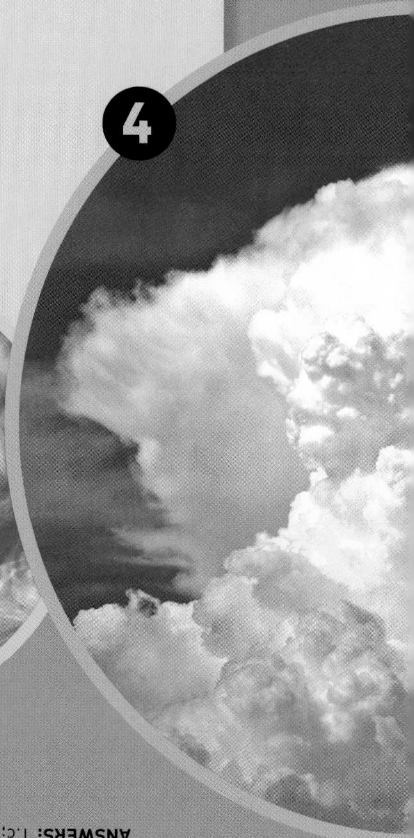

ANSWERS: 1.c; 2.b; 3.d; 4.a

	Rainfall	Temperature	Barometric Pressure	Type of Clouds
Monday	0.0 in	90°F (32.2°C)	30.00 in (1015.9 millibars)	cumulus
Tuesday	.25 in (.63 cm)	87°F (30.5°C)	29.77 in (1008.1 millibars)	stratus
Wednesday				
Thursday				
Friday				

BE A LOCAL WEATHER-WATCHER!

For the next two weeks, keep track of the weather in your neighborhood. You will need a notebook or journal, a coffee can, a ruler, an outdoor thermometer, and access to the Internet. First, set up a chart like the one shown above.

To measure rainfall, place a small coffee can outside in an unsheltered place. Use a ruler to measure the amount of rain captured in the can. Record the outdoor temperature shown on the thermometer. Log on to the local weather station's website to find out the day's barometric pressure. At the end of two weeks, look at your chart. What patterns do you discover?

WEATHER ALERT IN JAPAN, TYPHOONS ARE GIVEN NUMBERS INSTEAD OF NAMES.

PREPARING FOR THE WEATHER

THE WEATHER FORECAST SAYS

THAT A STORM IS ON THE WAY. Quick, what do you do? When severe weather is headed in your direction, it is important to make like a scout and be prepared. During bad weather, you might have to make some big decisions. But weather is also an excuse to have some fun. Try these weather-related activities.

SNOW DAY?
YOU BE THE JUDGE

You wake up in the morning and find an inch of snow on the ground. You are the superintendent of schools, so you have to make an important decision. Should you declare a snow day? Here are the facts to consider:

- There is 1 inch (2.5 cm) of snow on the ground, and 2 more inches (5 cm) are expected today.
- Roadway conditions are icy.
- Eighty percent of students use bus transportation to get to school.
- Fifty percent of teachers travel from other towns.
- Today is the day for state math tests.
- You have already used three of the four snow days allowed for the year.

Should you call a snow day? Think about the pros and cons.

PROS It's a snow day! You get the day off. Everybody gets to stay home where it's warm and safe.

CONS You have to make up missed state tests, and you've been preparing for them for weeks. Also, you can't afford to use up all your snow days.

WHAT'S YOUR DECISION?
IS IT A SNOW DAY?

ANSWER: Most school officials would err on the side of safety, call the snow day, and reschedule the test.

MAKE AN EMERGENCY KIT

As the old saying goes, "It's better to be safe than sorry." Having a severe weather emergency kit on hand is a good way to prepare for storms. A kit will be especially helpful if your home loses power. Here is a list of what you might need, for one person, for up to seven days. Pack your kit and keep it ready.

- at least 1 gallon (3.8 l) of water per day
- blankets
- clothing
- toiletries (soap, toothpaste)
- a first-aid kit
- flashlights
- radio
- batteries
- charged cell phone
- canned or packaged foods
- games, books, chocolate

You need the essential items, but don't forget about the fun stuff, too. Some sweet treats and toys or games will help you ride out the storm.

IS THIS BUILDING READY FOR A STORM?

Look at this picture. Think about how someone might prepare for severe weather, such as a hurricane or tornado. Do you think this driveway and house are ready for a storm? Which objects listed in the box below would you need to move, close, or bring inside in order to get ready for a big storm? Use the sentences below to help you figure out where to safely store these things during the storm.

bicycle	boxes
flowerpot	backpack
sports equipment	pets
mower	garage door

I WOULD—
1. close the _____ .
2. cover the _____ with a tarp.
3. move the _____ into the garage.
4. bring the _____ inside the house.

ANSWERS: 1. garage door; 2. flowerpot; 3. bicycle, sports equipment, mower; 4. pets, backpack, boxes

WEATHER ALERT   OBJECTS BLOWN ABOUT IN TWISTERS HAVE BEEN DISCOVERED MILES AWAY FROM WHERE THEY STARTED.

WEATHER
MYTHS VS. FACTS

CAN YOU GUESS WHICH
SAYINGS ARE MYTHS AND WHICH ARE FACTS?

A When birds line up on a telephone wire, expect rain.

B When cows lie down in a field, bad weather is coming.

C When bees seek shelter, rain will follow.

D When seagulls fly back over land, rain may be on its way.

E When dogs eat grass, expect a severe storm.

F When pigs gather leaves and straw, a storm is coming.

A MYTH. There is no proven link between birds roosting on wires and the weather. Truth is, if there are lots of birds and lots of wires in a particular area, birds will rest there. Migrating birds might sense a drop in barometric pressure and decide to wait out a bad storm, however.

B MYTH. There are a number of possible reasons that cows lie down in a field. Cows tend to lie down when they are chewing their cud. Or they might just be tired! During a storm, cows are more likely to seek shelter under a tree.

WEATHER ALERT GROUNDHOG DAY COMES FROM A SIMILAR GERMAN TRADITION INVOLVING HEDGEHOGS.

C **FACT.** Bees do appear to sense a decrease in barometric pressure. The fine hairs on their backs pick up on building electrostatic pressure in rain clouds. When this happens, they retreat to their hives to avoid raindrops that are almost as big as they are. So when bees beat a retreat, it's time to take cover!

IS GROUNDHOG DAY FOR REAL?

Each February 2, Americans pause with excitement for a weather report from a groundhog named Punxsutawney Phil. According to tradition, if the groundhog sees its shadow, expect six more weeks of winter. If it does not see its shadow, then spring is almost here. Can groundhogs really predict the weather? Not so much. Since 1887, Punxsutawney Phil has been correct just 39 percent of the time. Groundhog Day is really just an excuse to put on a show in Punxsutawney, Pennsylvania, with a groundhog as the star. Air masses, wind currents, moisture in the air, and a host of other factors determine the weather, not Phil. But you already knew that.

D **FACT.** Birds also can sense when the air pressure drops. Seagulls don't like flying during heavy winds, so they will stop flying over water and turn inland when a storm is on its way. If you are on the beach and suddenly there are more seagulls on the sand than beachgoers, it might be time to head indoors.

E **MYTH.** All dogs eat grass from time to time, and it has nothing to do with the weather. Sometimes they do it for the same reason humans enjoy a salad—to add variety to their diets. Other times, they chew grass when they have upset stomachs. However, their taste for leafy greens has nothing to do with the weather.

IT'S ALL GREEK TO ME

Just about every culture has mythological stories about the weather. Long ago, people believed that gods and goddesses controlled the sky, water, air, and weather. They used these stories to explain weather events in a time before scientific knowledge. The ancient Greeks believed that Zeus was the god of clouds, rain, thunder, and lightning. Iris was the goddess of the rainbow who carried messages for the gods. Write your own mythological story about a weather event.

F **MYTH.** Pigs have a strong nesting instinct. Straw, leaves, and other soft vegetation are favorite nesting materials. Some pigs feel this instinct more strongly than others, regardless of the weather forecast.

PICTURE THE WEATHER

HEY, WEATHER EXPERT! YOU KNOW BY NOW THAT WEATHER IS EVERY-WHERE. You have to deal with it, like it or not. It affects what you wear. And sometimes you can't even escape the weather when you watch a movie!

WHAT IN THE WORLD?

Can you guess the weather gear shown in these extreme close-ups?

1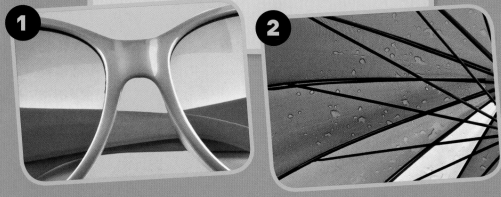

2

3

4

5

6

7

8

9

ANSWERS: 1. sunglasses; 2. umbrella; 3. raincoat; 4. boots; 5. glove; 6. snow hat; 7. parka; 8. baseball hat (to shield from sun); 9. bathing suit

WEATHER ALERT
THERE ARE MORE THAN 200 POP SONGS WITH WEATHER-RELATED WORDS IN THE TITLES.

WEATHER IN THE MOVIES

Weather adds drama to any movie, but is it realistic? Sometimes filmmakers ignore science or use special effects to create wild weather.

THE WIZARD OF OZ

How did the filmmakers in 1939 make a tornado that landed a house on top of a wicked witch? They built a 35-foot (11 m) cloth sock. The top was hung from the top of the stage while the bottom disappeared into a slot on the floor. By moving both ends of the sock in different directions, stagehands made the tornado look like it was moving back and forth. An image of a tornado was projected onto a screen while the actors stood in front of it and wind machines blew dried leaves. At $12,000, it was the most expensive special effect in the movie.

CLOUDY WITH A CHANCE OF MEATBALLS

To create the food in this computer-animated film, the makers got their hands dirty. First, they took real food and threw it off rooftops to see what it looked like as it fell. What a mess! Then they made models from clay and used special lighting to make the food look good enough to eat. Animators created 80 different kinds of food, including hamburgers, gelatin, and of course, meatballs.

PERCY JACKSON & THE LIGHTNING THIEF

To create this movie's *electrifying* lightning scenes, with actors flying above the Empire State Building, moviemakers took photographs of New York City and combined them into a computer-generated background. The actors filmed the scenes in the studio, flying on wires. Special effects experts then used computers to merge the shots of the actors with the background and added animated lightning.

TWISTER

Almost 60 years after *The Wizard of Oz* came out, filmmakers used computers instead of socks for special effects. A special-effects company developed software that could create and light individual dust particles in the tornado from different angles. To create the debris that flew around during storms, the filmmakers used computer technology as well as an airplane engine to blow stuff around. *Twister* has become the standard for computerized special effects.

PHOTO FINISH

STORM CHASING BY TIM SAMARAS

CHASING STORMS HAS

BECOME A WAY OF LIFE, BUT IT NEVER GETS OLD. This shot was taken on May 29, 2004, at about 6:30 p.m. I was with my crew in southern Sumner County, which is located in south-central Kansas, close to the border of Oklahoma.

It's amazing to be close to a tornado like this—all your senses come alive! You can hear the wind roar past you and see details of the tornado that remain invisible only a mile or so away. This was an incredible day. There were five other tornadoes that came out of this same thunderstorm. This tornado was the most spectacular, but we saw others that were more than one-quarter mile wide (0.4 km). When we tried to follow one other large tornado that day, it kept dropping debris and trees in our path, so it was difficult to keep up. We had to get out of our vehicle several times to move power poles out of our way!

It is common to be this close to a tornado when we are out in the field. We place instruments in the path of tornadoes, so we have to get close to make sure we get a direct hit. We've actually been closer to a storm than this one.

Tornado forecasting can be very difficult. The best scientists in the world can't tell you exactly where tornadoes will be, even when conditions are good. The ingredients have to be perfect for a tornado to form. This is where our research comes in. We collect measurements inside and outside the funnel clouds to help us understand them better. Information about air pressure, temperature, humidity, wind speed, and wind direction help us learn about the environments that are best for tornadoes—and why they get so powerful.

AFTERWORD

REBUILDING AFTER A STORM

A DEADLY TORNADO

STRUCK THE TOWN OF GREENSBURG,
Kansas, on May 4, 2007. The twister rated an EF-5 on the Fujita scale, with winds of more than 205 miles per hour (330 kph). Eleven people were killed, and about 95 percent of the town's buildings were leveled to the ground. The other five percent were severely damaged. The tornado was larger than the entire town itself, with swirling winds 1.7 miles wide (2.7 km).

The people of Greensburg had no choice but to rebuild from top to bottom. Instead of letting the devastating storm ruin their spirits, however, the people decided to take the town's name to heart. They rebuilt their town as a "green," or environmentally friendly community. They followed better environmental standards and building codes than the law required. All buildings larger than 4,000 square feet were built to the highest level of a building standard, called the Leadership in Energy and Environmental Design or LEED. For a town this size, Greensburg now has the most eco-friendly buildings in the world.

The new buildings have stronger, energy-efficient windows, which allow in natural light and cut down on energy use. The energy that powers the new buildings comes from renewable sources, instead of fossil fuels, which pollute the atmosphere. Solar and wind energy keep the new town running.

Greensburg stands today as a model for other communities that have been devastated by severe weather and must be rebuilt. The people of Greensburg have shown that it is possible to lose everything and then rebuild with a positive view of the future. The town's new slogan is, "Rebuilding . . . Stronger, Better, Greener!"

In 2007, an EF-5 tornado leveled the town of Greensburg, Kansas.

Rebuilding the town gave people a chance to use sustainable energy and eco-friendly building materials.

Turbines harness the power of the wind to provide electricity for the residents of Greensburg.

Not all weather sends people scurrying indoors. A sunny fall day can bring friends together.

AN INTERACTIVE GLOSSARY

Strong winds fill the colorful sails of these racing boats.

THESE WORDS ARE
COMMONLY USED BY METEOROLOGISTS when
they talk about the weather. Use the glossary to learn what each word means and visit its page numbers to see the word used in context. Then test your weather knowledge!

Atmospheric pressure
(PAGES 12–13)
The pressure caused by the weight of the atmosphere

It might rain if the atmospheric pressure _____.
a. falls
b. rises
c. sways
d. stays the same

Cirrus
(PAGES 14–15)
Thin, wispy tufts of clouds that hang high in the atmosphere

What are cirrus clouds made of?
a. wind
b. ice crystals
c. warm water
d. sand

Condense
(PAGES 18–19)
To change from a gas, or vapor, to a liquid

What kind of air makes water vapor condense?
a. moist
b. warm
c. cool
d. windy

Cumulonimbus
(PAGES 14–15)
Tall, dark clouds with rising air currents

What kind of weather might follow cumulonimbus clouds?
a. sunny
b. rainy
c. hot
d. foggy

Cumulus
(PAGES 14–15)
White, fluffy clouds with lots of blue sky between them

What kind of weather might follow a cumulus cloud?
a. sunny
b. rainy
c. hot
d. foggy

Evaporate
(PAGES 18–19)
To change from a liquid to a gas, or vapor

Which kind of air causes water on land or in the atmosphere to evaporate?
a. moist
b. warm
c. cool
d. windy

Haboob
(PAGES 38–39)
A dust storm caused by sudden downdrafts that loosen desert sand

What is another word for a haboob?
a. beachhead
b. thunderclap
c. spiral arm
d. sandstorm

Occluded front
(PAGES 36–37)
Lines on a weather map that show where one air mass takes over another

Occluded fronts show where weather will _____.
a. change
b. stay the same
c. become cold
d. become snowy

Precipitation
(PAGES 16–17)
Water that falls from the atmosphere to the ground as part of the water cycle

Which is NOT an example of precipitation?
a. rain
b. snow
c. lightning
d. sleet

Storm surge
(PAGES 20–21)
A rise in sea level that occurs due to changes in atmospheric pressure and winds

Which type of storm usually causes a storm surge?
a. hurricane
b. tornado
c. blizzard
d. thunderstorm

Stratus
(PAGES 14–15)
Thick clouds that hang low and cover the sky

Which weather condition could stratus clouds cause?
a. hail
b. snow
c. fog
d. wind

Supercell
(PAGES 24–25)
Powerful, rotating thunderstorm

Which type of weather is most likely to form from a supercell?
a. drought
b. tornado
c. hurricane
d. flood

Troposphere
(PAGES 12–13)
The lowest layer of the atmosphere

Which occurs in the troposphere?
a. wind
b. precipitation
c. clouds
d. all of the above

Hot, sunny days call for a refreshing dip in the pool.

Answers: Atmospheric pressure: a; Cirrus: b; Condense: c; Cumulonimbus: b; Cumulus: a; Evaporate: b; Haboob: d; Occluded front: a; Precipitation: c; Storm surge: a; Stratus: c; Supercell: b; Troposphere: d

FIND OUT MORE

Chase down more facts about weather with these websites, games, and books.

WEATHER SITES

education.noaa.gov/
A site prepared by NOAA (National Oceanic and Atmospheric Administration), the leading organization in tracking weather and providing warnings

spaceplace.nasa.gov/planet-weather/en/
All about weather, on Earth and throughout the solar system

theweatherchannelkids.com/
A website designed to teach kids about the weather, climate, and preparing for the weather

WEATHER GAMES

Interactive Weather Maker
Control atmospheric conditions and be your own weather maker. To play, visit **scholastic.com/kids/weather.**

National Geographic Kids Brainteaser: Tornado
To play a fun tornado trivia game, visit National Geographic Kids online at **kids.nationalgeographic.com/kids/games/geographygames/brainteasertornado.**

DVDS TO WATCH

"Stormageddon"
National Geographic, 2011

"Tornado Intercept"
National Geographic, 2005

WEATHER BOOKS

The Kids' Book of Weather Forecasting
By Mark Breen and Kathleen Friestad
Ideals, 2008
Descriptions of weather events, with kid-friendly activities

Tornado Hunter: Getting Inside the Most Violent Storms on Earth
By Stefan Bechtel and Tim Samaras
National Geographic, 2009
Like the deadly tornadoes this book documents, this potent combination of high adventure and hard science is timely in our era of global warming and climate change.

Witness to Disaster: Drought
By Dennis and Judith Fradin
National Geographic Children's Books, 2008
This history of droughts around the world compares impacts on a wide variety of societies.

Witness to Disaster: Hurricanes
By Dennis and Judith Fradin
National Geographic Children's Books, 2007
Step into the eye of the storm. Follow the action, from the first news reports of a hurricane called Katrina gathering out at sea, to eyewitness accounts of survivors in the aftermath of the storm.

To my father, Charles Suter, a dedicated teacher who always loved the great outdoors. –KF

Acknowledgments: Special thanks to Stephanie A. Weiss, Research Associate at the Cooperative Institute for Mesoscale Meteorological Studies at the University of Oklahoma, and Tim Samaras, National Geographic Emerging Explorer

Published by the National Geographic Society

John M. Fahey, Jr., *Chairman of the Board and Chief Executive Officer*
Timothy T. Kelly, *President*
Declan Moore, *Executive Vice President; President, Publishing*
Melina Gerosa Bellows, *Executive Vice President; Chief Creative Officer, Books, Kids, and Family*

Prepared by the Book Division

Hector Sierra, *Senior Vice President and General Manager*
Nancy Laties Feresten, *Senior Vice President, Editor in Chief, Children's Books*
Jonathan Halling, *Design Director, Books and Children's Publishing*
Jay Sumner, *Director of Photography, Children's Publishing*
Jennifer Emmett, *Editorial Director, Children's Books*
Eva Absher-Schantz, *Managing Art Director*
Carl Mehler, *Director of Maps*
R. Gary Colbert, *Production Director*
Jennifer A. Thornton, *Managing Editor*

Staff for This Book

Robin Terry, *Project Editor*
Lori Epstein, *Senior Illustrations Editor*
Grace Hill, *Associate Managing Editor*
Joan Gossett, *Production Editor*
Lewis R. Bassford, *Production Manager*
Susan Borke, *Legal and Business Affairs*
Kate Olesin, *Assistant Editor*
Kathryn Robbins, *Design Production Assistant*
Hillary Moloney, *Illustrations Assistant*

Manufacturing and Quality Management

Christopher A. Liedel, *Chief Financial Officer*
Phillip L. Schlosser, *Senior Vice President*
Chris Brown, *Technical Director*
Nicole Elliott, *Manager*
Rachel Faulise, *Manager*
Robert L. Barr, *Manager*

Design and Production by Bill Smith Group, partnered with Q2Amedia

Captions

Page 1: An elk in Yukon Territory, Canada, peers out from a forest covered in hoar frost—patterns of tiny ice crystals that form on freezing cold surfaces.
Pages 2–3: The sun sets dramatically over the Seychelles, islands off the coast of Africa.

The National Geographic Society is one of the world's largest nonprofit scientific and educational organizations. Founded in 1888 to "increase and diffuse geographic knowledge," the Society works to inspire people to care about the planet. National Geographic reflects the world through its magazines, television programs, films, music and radio, books, DVDs, maps, exhibitions, live events, school publishing programs, interactive media and merchandise. *National Geographic* magazine, the Society's official journal, published in English and 33 local-language editions, is read by more than 38 million people each month. The National Geographic Channel reaches 320 million households in 34 languages in 166 countries. National Geographic Digital Media receives more than 15 million visitors a month. National Geographic has funded more than 9,400 scientific research, conservation and exploration projects and supports an education program promoting geography literacy.

For more information, please call 1-800-NGS LINE (647-5463), visit nationalgeographic.com, or write to the following address:
National Geographic Society
1145 17th Street N.W.
Washington, D.C. 20036-4688 U.S.A.

Visit us online at nationalgeographic.com/books

For librarians and teachers: ngchildrensbooks.org

More for kids from National Geographic:
kids.nationalgeographic.com

For information about special discounts for bulk purchases, please contact National Geographic Books Special Sales: ngspecsales@ngs.org

For rights or permissions inquiries, please contact National Geographic Books Subsidiary Rights: ngbookrights@ngs.org

Library of Congress Cataloging-in-Publication Data

Furgang, Kathy. Weather : facts, photos, and fun that will blow you away / by Kathy Furgang.
p. cm. — (National Geographic kids. Everything)
Includes bibliographical references and index.
ISBN 978-1-4263-1063-8 (lib. bdg.) —
ISBN 978-1-4263-1058-4 (pbk.)
1. Weather—Juvenile literature. I. Title. QC981.3.F87
2012 551.6—dc23

2011035772

Scholastic ISBN: 978-1-4263-1004-1

Printed in the United States of America
13/WOR/2